T0151095

Folding Ruler Star

Poems

<u>Aaron Kunin</u>

Published in the United States by
Fence Books
303 East Eighth Street, #B1
New York, NY 10009
www.fencebooks.com

Cover diagram by Sarah Oppenheimer

Frontispiece photograph,
Bamboostange Liebt Zollstockstern
(Bamboo Pole Loves Folding Ruler Star),
15 black-and-white photographs,
1968–1969 by Sigmar Polke, courtesy
of Walker Art Center, Minneapolis

Book design by Mark Owens

Fence Books are distributed by
University Press of New England
www.upne.com

Fence Books are printed in Canada by
Westcan Printing Group
www.westcanpg.com

Library of Congress Cataloguing in Publication Data
Kunin, Aaron [1973–]
Folding Ruler Star / Aaron Kunin

Library of Congress Control Number: 2005923085

ISBN 0-9740909-8-0

First Edition

Contents

Preface

These poems are conceived as a value-neutral *Paradise Lost*. In other words, someone who is not god tells you to avoid a certain tree, and you disobey the instruction; the result is shame.

Two characters agree that one of them is supposed to worship and obey the other without actually believing that the other possesses any special qualities that would enforce obedience; the first one disobeys the second one and has to be punished.

A body has five parts; each part is alarmed. Descriptions of the parts set off the alarms.

Affect lives in the face and is measured with a ruler.

The measure is a five-syllable line arranged in three-line units. Each poem is mirrored by another poem with the same title.

Some of these poems have appeared in *Boog City, Carve, The D.C. Poetry Anthology 2003, Fence, No: A Journal of the Arts, The Poetry Project Newsletter, The Poker, Radical Society, Sal Mimeo, Spur,* and *War and Peace.*

These poems are for Jonathan Goldberg.

"The shame response is an act which reduces facial communication. It stands in the same relation to looking and smiling as silence stands to speech and as disgust, nausea, and vomiting stand to hunger and eating. By dropping his eyes, his eyelids, his head, and sometimes the whole upper part of his body, the individual calls a halt to looking at another person, particularly the other person's face, and to the other person's looking at him, particularly at his face."

Silvan Tomkins, *Affect, Imagery, Consciousness*

THE SHAME TREE

the t.v. has a
human face (the face
has two memories)

in the shade of low
branches or human
furniture under

the smothering tree
the damaged women
(enter together)

and some of them heard
(pretended not to
hear) your suffering

tree's facial nightlight
ripening human
(yes) fruits behind the

eyes tree looked thicker
reflected in your
hair ah in the shape-

less mask of your hair
your additional
hair your living hair

THE SHAME TREE

aspirin tonight
no contempt please no
contempt tonight please

FALSE NATIVITY

masking memory
(no current photo
available) with

furniture placement
(that memory has
two faces is true)

but what I saw then
terrified me (I
removed my glasses

I put them on the
desk) and the desk was
terrified

that I might sit on
my glasses and what
my bottom would see

FALSE NATIVITY

alliteration
perfectly masking
malevolence (that

malevolence has
faces is true) with
furniture placement

(inaudible to
itself) masking the
dent carved in the bridge

of your nose by your
glasses (no current
photo) masking in

analysis of
a human novel
the clock's machine heart

UNDER THE LAMPSHADE

his wild path around
the kitchen (afraid
that the light fixture

might clobber him if
he passed underneath)
to avoid crossing

under (her slicker
gave the effect of
a lampshade) lest the

light fixture alight
(every time she does
something to hurt him

she cries no stop you're
hurting me) on his
trembling shoulders and

now he kisses both
her real foot and her
artificial foot

UNDER THE LAMPSHADE

he punishes them
because he believes
he should be punished

(categorical
imperative) he
seems to be wearing

a lampshade in place
of a raincoat (he
wants to bite his tail

it's just out of reach)
and afraid (should the
fixture come unfixed)

the light from the
hanging lantern might
fall like the human

fruit when you close your
lips around its toe
and pull and (afraid

he'll touch the burning
bulb to his face) and
it would leave a mark

HIDDEN SCHOOL ENTRANCE

takes us back to the
scene remembered by
the phrase (five years have

passed) because they had
not been per-fec-ted
(five syllables with

the length of five long
winters) and again
(this is not a bill

do not pay this) a
truck pulls up to the
library to fill

the Pepsi machines
circles the building
and enters at the

(and earth exalted
on its center hung)
vulnerable back

HIDDEN SCHOOL ENTRANCE

misguided moral
(happiness without
work) and aesthetic

principles replaced
by misguided (pays
without entering)

economic (chews
without swallowing)
principles (for

the lies in the books
in our collection
we apologize)

LOST AMBULANCES

to a pain affix
a voice (books stop
lying) remembered

by the phrase splashing
through the unseen mud
and (never the same

color) as the road
beyond unfolds like
a truth (in human

syllables) what was
splashing in that child-
like receptive soul

(little forgotten
bookmark) alive in
painful memory

LOST AMBULANCES

a kiss on the eye
and it's the knife that
bleeds (only because

your body's sharper
than any knife) and
the mirror itself

drools (one thread of drool
connects mirror to
you) at the promise

of human food and
whispers (inhuman
syllables) find out

what they eat and give
it to them (testing
is now painless but

expensive) as the
skull rejects the face
tasted like apple

(triumph of money
over pain) I have
tasted like apple

FOOD SYNTAX

I could eat you (smiles
reassuringly
at his own image

reflected in the
sexual mirror)
with a spoon (merely

the nicest thing you've
ever said to me)
or is it better

to be eaten with
knife and fork (better
than with a spoon)

FOOD SYNTAX

my hands seek out new
textures (he often
imagined stabbing

himself in the eye)
for example with
a pen (scooping them

out with a grapefruit
spoon or otherwise
de-eyeing himself

etcetera) I
am always happy
because I have a

razor hidden in
my face (that part casts
a shadow over

the following part
get rid of that part
the next part appears

different) it takes the
place of the removed
(do you eat the head

first) I am always
happy because I
eat at Schneider's Grill

THE SHAME WORD

warm milk at bedtime
and crackers (glimmer
of light through pen cap)

from the mineral
kingdom (destined to
have every affect

totally bound by
shame) we proudly serve
(milk and crackers your

highness) the one thing
she can refuse (small
vacuum in pen cap)

it's only the most
unfair thing you can
do to a person

but the double bind
is only double
(releasing a green

dye into the air
of her own comforts)
it does not bind (her

THE SHAME WORD

refusal) to serve
(milk and crackers your
harness) producing

a total affect
shame bind (not allowed
to be powerless

we can't even have
no response) and it's
the knife that's holding

us together tree
one should color one's
life should dye it green

tree (bred for shadow)
so many things could
be replaced by this

tree (no more new pens)
with a face from the
mineral kingdom

GRIEF ACT ABSENT SOURCE

exposed wrist (try to
hide that) you like it
between the sleeve (and

the glove) only the
glove did not have its
own sleeve (you'll see it

terminate almost
successfully) in
flesh (process laid bare

the shirt of purple
wool and bodysuit)
exposing only

the feet and the tips
of the fingers the
neck and the head and

with zippers (closures)
you can't deny that
(with each viewing the

face dies one last time)
you like it between
grief (act absent) source

GRIEF ACT ABSENT SOURCE

after three hours (one
can only smile when
one looks at this) this

morning in front of
the mirror (pulling
off the glove finger

by finger) you're two
hours late and the sweep
of (violent rain

had denuded the
trees) your corduroy
placed between (grief act

absent source) the thick
cords and the lining
(and the creases are

indescribable
lips wrapping this
body in a sheet

of kisses) from which
you're almost success-
fully divided

.

SMILE WHEN YOU LOOK AT

when the sky is ice
dark when the insect's
back shines like a watch

face (six o'clock) glazed
in silver lightning
when learning to kiss

the back of the hand
rather than the palm
(when the only sane

response is fear) when
Christ demands (with a
perceptible shake

at the ends of his
fingers) why have you
forsaken me is

it a quotation
when (from its hiding
place does a smile flow

over the lower
half of your face) when
you remove the knife

SMILE WHEN YOU LOOK AT

at the lecture hall
at the hidden school
(curious faces

of the listeners
alternately blocked
and viewed over and

behind and around
his emphatically
bobbing head) in air

suspended (locked in
a beautifully
renovated late

nineteenth century
house with a backyard)
written in English

ACCESS DENIED

shame went walking (by
evening it was cool
enough) to seed with

mistakes (if moral
variety is
what you're looking for

you're in the wrong place)
you're not supposed to
you're supposed to want

to (either you want
them to or you want
only to punish

them for) avoiding
consistently the
drinking fountain on

the floor where he worked
in accordance with
secret principles

ACCESS DENIED

this magazine is
the wrong place (if you're
looking for moral

variety) you
need only put out
your hand (don't touch it

don't look at it) for
moral symmetry
(not realizing

when you touch in one
place that you're really
touching all over)

GIRL AND REPTILE

and reptile made a
gesture as if to
tantalize her with

the money as if
(if the girl was not
going to take it

immediately)
it should be kept just
out of her reach and

girl made a gesture
as if polishing
the spectacles on

her thigh as if (since
she wanted his sight
to be directed

downwards) his gaze (the
direction of his
face) was in the way

GIRL AND REPTILE

and girl turns toward
the accident with
an expectant look

as if it had been
a deliberate
attempt to gain her

attention (her tongue
wiping the shredded
inside of her cheek)

and would you eat the
apple (again she
finds herself on the

phone yelling at a
stranger) I would peel
and core the apple

yes little brother
(her face contorted
and her tongue pressing

against her cheek caused
it to bulge) you shall
have an apple too

SEXUAL SHOCK

someone's weakness not
my own movement from
my nervous and self-

destructive self to
your leg (to your knee
let's say) is the same

as machines unzip
concrete dividers
on the highway is

this self-protecting
(body's protecting
itself but the voice

isn't) the same two
zipper toggles from
someone's body not

my own (arm folded
in the hollow of
the neck) in what sense

SEXUAL SHOCK

is it a knife (the
same as a person)
whose eyes were slash marks

whose body quivered
with sexual shock
(collaboration

with sexual shock
inflicted on the
roof of a building

on a stairwell) wedged
in the car door the
body's protecting

itself from what (is
this the same as self-
protection) the voice

is saying what new
buildings are scheduled
for demolition

ZIPDOWN DAY

I don't like to eat
when I'm aroused (an
excuse to repeat

an action) closing
his eyes as though to
keep from crying as

though in a state of
arousal (as though
overcome by an

emotion without
appearing to them)
the room seemed larger

(furrowing his brow)
as though trying to
concentrate (eating

as though amused by
holding the paper
at a right angle

ZIPDOWN DAY

in the absence of
any affect) the
room seemed larger (like

an apple dully
shining) producing
a number from its

center the room seemed
larger (if you stand
that's perceived as a

threat) withdrawing your
look (as though in a
state of arousal

as though trying to
concentrate) because
I've always been slow

to get undressed the
room seemed larger as
though in a state of

FACESITTING

arousal (partly
obscured by a hand
held instrument of

gratification)
stuck to the mirror
(on the sensitive

side) of the upturned
face of a doll with
human mouth and (eyes

powerfully closed)
in submission to
a doll whose foot is

a knife (folded to
keep from touching the
neck) positioning

the device in the
assumed direction
of its mouth (put your

finger in it to
hear again the same
words) to prick its face

FACESITTING

sitting ghost (partly
obscured by a hand
held microphone) at

least you can still breathe
through your eyes (only
your anatomy

was missing) slowly
turn your head and be
gratified (enraged

aroused) degraded
and absent (pencil)
razed lightly (scratch scratch

rub rub) rubbing to
ill effect among
the missing products

FIVE SECURITY ZONES

colorful inside
of the mouth is the
first zone freestanding

hair is the second
zone a mask of phone
and coffee is the

third zone (that you are
forced to correspond
with) the fourth zone is

the almost complete
absence of demands
for reassurance

in your speech the fifth
zone is the shining
mass behind the eyes

FIVE SECURITY ZONES

point of a building's
shadow enters you
Ferdinand Lopez

(are you carrying
anything that will
set off the alarm)

at Tenway Junction
(the security
guard sees that you have

no destination)
through a cloud choking
the sky's mouth minus

(smashed into bloody
atoms) his face said
get back on the train

FIVE SECURITY ZONES

ends of the mouth turned
down (at its center
it indented) and

pouted (a frown of
satisfaction) and
the spaces between

the parted lips the
eyelid and the edge
of the eye as well

as the space under
the nose seemed to be
open to admit

most of the bites some
of the chews all of
the swallows (take note

FIVE SECURITY ZONES

and speaking of (looks
to avoid) the pain
of self-exposure

until (avoidance
becomes painful) the
back of the chair blocks

view of her plate bowl
glass (but rising and
descending spoons grant

one an idea
of what's behind) at
which your shield becomes

a burden (your shield)
reading a book is
cutting off the head

FIVE SECURITY ZONES

mouth is a castle
for defending an
idea (at each

level the worst threat
to security
defines the next zone)

at each level the
mouth emits a shrill
repeating alarm

(I walk by and don't
even notice and
finally I do)

are you carrying
anything that hides
or alters women

FIVE SECURITY ZONES

different creature
(you get a glimpse in
the way he removes

his coat and folds it
neatly of what he
might look like fully

undressed if he got
so involved in the
act he forgot to

stop removing and
folding until he
had exposed himself)

in front of the school
dragonflies emerge
from their backpacks

FIVE SECURITY ZONES

although (forgiveness
means removing the
division) simply

being human is
not (no that is not
unforgivable)

enough (a female
must sit on its grave)
to penetrate the

first zone is (although
not a strong enough
advocate of your

desire) although the
security you
bring is an insult

FIVE SECURITY ZONES

a mask of phone and
coffee (but it's the
lowest part of the

head that suffers the
taste of your own mask)
would disgust strangers

approaching making
scissoring gestures
(what are the limits

of division) in
Baltimore by the
shape of the Safeway

(divisible by
five) the front end of
the brain receives light

YOU APPEAR TO BE
USING A VERSION
OF TELNET SOFTWARE

WHICH IS NOT SECURE
THE INFORMATION
THAT YOU SEND CAN BE

READ WHILE IN TRANSIT
STARTING APRIL 9
2001

THIS SYSTEM WILL NO
LONGER RECOGNIZE
ANY INSECURE

CONNECTIONS APRIL
9 HAS PASSED UPGRADE
IMMEDIATELY

SHOW AN ALERT WHEN
SUBMITTING A FORM
WHICH IS NOT SECURE

FIVE SECURITY ZONES

Baltimore (set your
watch back ten minutes)
I will never cry

in front of the school
(put it in writing
written messages

save time and avoid
errors) by the shape
of the Safeway in

handing out words not
money (the more you
give him the more he

cries) depending on
what side of the face
you're trying to hide

FIVE SECURITY ZONES

first zone is although
the revisions have
drawn blood (his eye peeled

off with the bandage)
from the tomb on which
(the security

guard stands) sits hides or
alters a woman's
shape in words of one

syllable (but none
of the syllables
was secure) I work

for the C I A
I'm not a spy I
just read books

FIVE SECURITY ZONES

sleep secure with our
surveillance ball (glazed
in silver lightning)

at the lecture hall
on a golden chain
the absent (pencil

the one instrument
I never use) one
should always fly at

half-mast (in words of
one syllable oh
but one of the words

was tender like a
bruise) dear diary
there's one thing I love

FIVE SECURITY ZONES

much as a single
shining hair driven
through the skin (how can

you call it a knife)
or stuck to the roof
of a mouth or of

a building (a lock
of your hair catches
the window as you

enter) or your hair
(shining mass of) as
a totality

or totality
itself (Aaron I
got the keys buzz up)

FIVE SECURITY ZONES

never put on your
blindfold (unfold and
study but do not

put it on) affix
it to your eyes do
not tighten ever

frequently try it
on never wear it
outside (I've never

seen it on him) at
any rate (they are
longing to wear it

secretly) for those
in peril do not
oh do not take it

FIVE SECURITY ZONES

of those swallows) first
stop train in tunnel
(all doors will open

to let off the ghosts
of those swallows) you
have now erased all

the information
(concerning the knife
paint won't dry on it

soap won't lather and
sandwiched between two
layers of thickly

spread peanut butter
this sandwich can't be
held) that doesn't cut

FIVE SECURITY ZONES

progress has become
a centipede (up
your back the backpack

advances on its
belly) until it
coats the spine (always

the same direction)
as a person you
can think it (what makes

you think I want to
touch it) through a cloud
subvocally the

sky's mouth said even
the sun gets lost in
this neighborhood

FIVE SECURITY ZONES

syllable is the
first zone boundary
must be crossed (again

please stop using the
word elliptical)
line is the second

zone (this word is re-
configurable)
parenthesis is

the third zone paper
is the fourth zone with-
(a security

blanket to sleep with)
drawing into your
book is the fifth zone

THE BLOODY REVISIONS

until the blood dried
and blackened he tried
unsuccessfully

(several times) to
masturbate and failed
(there's no way I could

possibly write that)
in the first person
keep the bristles hard

and brush teeth until
bloody (scratch out rub
out) hold smile until

bloody and (you know
how it can make you
want to roll in it

and do that sweet thing)
until it coats the
mirror properly

only for the warm
sleepy feeling it
gives you afterwards

THE BLOODY REVISIONS

wipe it properly
with a handkerchief
(employees must wash

hands twice) rubbing to
ill effect until
the return ticket

spins around on the
slippery cover
of the paperback

to keep the blood in
(in the shade of an
animal enraged

aroused disgusted
and absent) the eye
travels to the edge

of its socket (a
different creature
from the back) cover

CARTE DU TENDRE

publishing has no
face (copies shriek when
confronted with their

originals) and
no body (bloated
undistinguished blank

books undistinguished
blank pages) except
the lower back and

the lower belly
(another parting
in the darkness of

the brain no ruined
face) smiles out of a
map of tender spots

CARTE DU TENDRE

on the bus going
home the prisoner
remembered his eye-

glasses (worry lines
materialize
above them) flashing

lights reflected in
the beer bottles (dream
that removes anger

phone call retrieves it)
and no lumpy face
buried in the wet

center of a tree
(in the bark hate lines
make it go with a

complete sentence) which
suffers the dreadful
pain of the copy

SILENCE WAS PLEASED

shame is also in
sleep (clouds eat into
buildings) cut through the

paint (thought cut further
into speech) putting
her foot on the stair

she makes a cut (stair
closing cancelled) with
a hand to expose

an interior
through writing (teaching
torment) messages

that have no future
no rest interval
(much remains to be

written about clouds)
no division no
further assistance

SILENCE WAS PLEASED

did I ever tell
you (knowing I had
not) did I ever

tell you (knowing that
someone else had told
you but not knowing

who had done it but
suspecting) because
either she told her

and we didn't see
or she told her in
a way we couldn't

see or one of them
knew without being
told or one of them

was lying or they
both were (I insist
we go no further)

PETTING IMPERSONAL

they decided to
be nice to him as
an experiment

and the result was
that they got aroused
they decided to

torture him as an
experiment and
the result was that

they got aroused (the
results they obtained
were inconclusive)

these poems express my
dissatisfaction
with sexual life

PETTING IMPERSONAL

umbrella handle
pops out of shoulder
bag and pencil (un-

likely instrument
of domination)
burns into the side

of a building (now
you're poking me in
the eye) to induce

sleep deprivation
(I hope there still is
a head injury

laboratory)
at the detention
center unprepared

you come in late you
drink Coke loud and used
the wrong edition

of the poem (sorry
professor) sorry
isn't good enough

FOLDING RULER STAR

draw a circle in
the mirror (inside
and outside are not

places) half the size
of your face a hinged
ruler is a good

enough mother (out
of sympathy) for
measuring the bridge

between parent and
child (in your forehead
an innocent knife

good enough to score
the brow with a star
tattoo) and just think

think of the haircut
I'm going to get
soon (yeah) soon enough

FOLDING RULER STAR

undisturbed (by the
ordinary wear
and tear of closing

and opening) is
this benign ruler
(framed in a pocket

mirror) a noun that
wanted so badly
to name it became

an adjective (fold
means the segments do
not separate in

a cut) akimbo
ruler I adapt
to you faithfully

(in gradually
diminishing love
for perhaps two years)

almost is a good
enough iambic
pentameter line

FOLDED ENVELOPE

let's go for a walk
(friend) let's keep talking
now that it's almost

three in the morning
(when she drops her glove
you are expected

to pick it up) you
slowly realize
(as the comb imparts

a suggestion of
malice to the hair)
in the hush of the

brain (rot from within
with a look) the doll
says put me down please

with that look (the way
it drops to the floor)
it's almost as though

you're letting go of
your own cigarette
and stepping on it

FOLDED ENVELOPE

(chairs) reshape his back
and fold him again
for their protection

accommodate him
(books) empty themselves
care for him support

him again (cuts) in
the line of his smile
afflict him lightly

(light) in which he reads
to live at the fold
where the discarded

exoskeleton
of the backpack sends
(this cigarette end

won't go out) still too
smiling his face was
(a dangerous toy

a toy bus chasing
a toy train) brandished
a new fiery sword

a sword to invest
expose up to the
hilt the burning hilt

ENCLOSED PLEASE FIND

a lost green binder
with bridge inspection
criteria (un-

fold celestial guide)
my incoherent
message (truer words

were never spoken)
in the mush of the
brain (in a morass

of shame) I adapt
to you faithfully
(because I make no

care) and the plumbing
works incessantly
violently and

ironically
and (literally
riding on wings of

lightning) an engorged
cloud suddenly un-
covers head and sky

ENCLOSED PLEASE FIND

solitary male
walking softly (on
those curiously

sensitive little
appendages they
have) so he won't feel

as much (frequent and
terrifying pains
on the surface) of

the machine (they can't
blush cry or love but
it's precisely in

blushing crying and
loving that they are
most machine-like) like

an apple that did
not ripen (astral
physiognomy)

kindly no human
face smiles out of a
folding ruler star

THIS BOOK WAS DAMAGED
BY AN UNKNOWN LIQUID
AND MOLD

AND IT HAS RECEIVED THE
FOLLOWING CONSERVATION
TREATMENT

DRY CLEANED
DISINFECTED
BOOK REPAIR (HINGE REPAIR)

6/10/96
MSEL PRESERVATION

some of the words are
underlined (only
they are important)

Fence Books was launched in 2001 as an extension of **FENCE**, a biannual journal of poetry, fiction, art and criticism that has a mission to redefine the terms of accessibility by publishing challenging writing distinguished by idiosyncrasy and intelligence rather than by allegiance with camps, schools, or cliques. It is part of our press's mission to support writers who might otherwise have difficulty being recognized because their work doesn't answer to either the mainstream or to recognizable modes of experimentation.

The Alberta Prize is an annual series administered by Fence Books in collaboration with the Alberta duPont Bonsal Foundation. The Alberta Prize offers publication of a first or second book of poems by a woman, as well as a five thousand dollar cash prize.

Our second prize series is the **Fence Modern Poets Series**. This contest is open to poets of either gender and at any stage in their career, and offers a one thousand dollar cash prize in addition to book publication.

For more information about either prize, visit our website at **www.fencebooks.com**, or send an SASE to: Fence Books/[Name of Prize], 303 East Eighth Street, #B1, New York, New York, 10009.

For more about *Fence,* visit **www.fencemag.com**.

Fence Books Titles

Folding Ruler Star   Aaron Kunin

povel   Geraldine Kim
                                       2005 FENCE MODERN POETS SERIES

A MAGIC BOOK   Sasha Steensen
                                                   2004 ALBERTA PRIZE

The Commandrine and Other Poems   Joyelle McSweeney

MACULAR HOLE   Catherine Wagner

The Opening Question   Prageeta Sharma
                                       2004 FENCE MODERN POETS SERIES

Sky Girl   Rosemary Griggs
                                                   2003 ALBERTA PRIZE

Nota   Martin Corless-Smith

APPREHEND   Elizabeth Robinson
                                       2003 FENCE MODERN POETS SERIES

Father of Noise   Anthony McCann

The Real Moon of Poetry and Other   Tina Brown Celona
Poems   2002 ALBERTA PRIZE

The Red Bird   Joyelle McSweeney
                                       2002 FENCE MODERN POETS SERIES

Can You Relax in My House   Michael Earl Craig

ZIRCONIA   Chelsey Minnis
                                                   2001 ALBERTA PRIZE

MISS AMERICA   Catherine Wagner